Cogne

Sondrio

Brianza

place tab
behind head

place
tab in
slit

Sondrio province,
Lombardy region

Cogne,
Valle d'Aosta region

Brianza district, Lombardy region

Plate 1

Peasant dresses from
provinces outside Rome

place tab
behind
neck

Frascati

cut on
broken
line

La tovaglia
headdress

place
tab
behind
neck

Naples

Frascati, Latium region

Naples, Campania region

Plate 2

Albanian settlers

E

S

E

E

cut on
broken line

S

Typical
man's costume

Taormina

Sicily region

Plate 3

Oliena

E

E

cut on
broken line

place sash
behind head

Stocking cap

S

S

S

cut on
broken
line

Oliena

Sardinia region

Osilo

Plate 4

place
tab
behind
neck

Quartu
Sant'Elena

Nuoro province,
known as the
"Switzerland
of Sardinia"

E

cut on
broken line

place sash
behind head

Stocking cap

E

S

Sardinia region

Plate 5

Calabria

Calabria region

Molise

Viù, Piedmont region

Boiano,
Molise region

Veneto

Herb-woman
from Veneto region

Plate 6

Emilia-Romagna

Pontremoli,
Tuscany region

Il mésero, a huge shawl
from the Liguria region

Pontremoli

place
tab
behind
neck

Emilia-Romagna region

Plate 7

Aviano,
Friuli–Venezia Giulia region

E

Aviano

Aviano

place tab in slit

E

S

Tyrolese costumes from
Trentino–Alto Adige region

Plate 8